BRITAIN IN PICTURES
THE BRITISH PEOPLE IN PICTURES

ENGLISH RIVERS AND CANALS

GENERAL EDITOR

W. J. TURNER

The Editor is most grateful to all those who have
so kindly helped in the selection of illustrations
especially to officials of the various public
Museums Libraries and Galleries and
to all others who have generously
allowed pictures and MSS
to be reproduced

ENGLISH
RIVERS AND CANALS

FRANK EYRE AND CHARLES HADFIELD

WITH
8 PLATES IN COLOUR
AND
19 ILLUSTRATIONS IN
BLACK AND WHITE

COLLINS · 14 ST. JAMES'S PLACE · LONDON
MCMXXXXV

PRODUCED BY
ADPRINT LIMITED LONDON

PRINTED IN GREAT BRITAIN BY
THE SUN ENGRAVING CO LTD LONDON AND WATFORD
ON MELLOTEX BOOK PAPER MADE
BY TULLIS RUSSELL & CO LTD MARKINCH SCOTLAND

LIST OF ILLUSTRATIONS

BLACK AND WHITE ILLUSTRATIONS

IT seems to me that all men love rivers. There is something about their smooth flowing which answers one of our deepest instincts, and stirs the wandering spirit in our blood more powerfully than anything else in nature. The quiet movement of water between its banks moves us more intimately than the great swell of the sea because it is an older and more familiar thing—so old that I cannot but think that the first man who ever wandered from his home, whether it was in a tree, or a cave, or from whatever hearth we sprang, was inspired to do so by watching a stream flowing. Rivers are of old an essential part of man's communal and national life. They provided the first transport, and the first boundaries; they dictated the sites of towns; and they were one of the first sources of power known to man.

These feelings are common to all men of all countries; for all men love rivers, just as (and for similar reasons) all men love home, domestic animals —and the smell of wood-smoke. But over and above these universal feelings, the English rivers have an individual and characteristic charm which is as compelling as it is difficult to analyse. I have loved them as long as I can remember loving anything, and yet the nearest I can get to conveying it is to say that, like England itself, they are small, and yet have had an influence upon the world's history out of all proportion to their size. This is saying little more than that I love them because they are English—and yet

7

what more is there to say ? We in this island have always an especial affection for the little things of life, which is at once our failure and our greatness. If you put an Englishman in the middle of five hundred miles of rolling countryside and told him that it was all his own, and none could disturb his possession, he would before long build himself a small compact home-stead in the middle of it, securely hedged in from the rest of his world, and call it home. This habit of thought, coupled with a passion for travel and exploration which I do not think it too fanciful to imagine owes much to the example of rivers, has made us a great colonising nation—but if the greatness is to continue the hedges must come down.

Meanwhile, there are the homes and the hedges, and on the other side of the hedge is almost certainly a stream—"a living river by the door." For whereas in most countries the rivers loved and venerated have been the great coursing waterways of continents, England has always been a country of little rivers. This whole island is so laced and threaded with a network of tiny streams and diminutive rivers that hardly anyone who has the energy to walk more than a mile from his door can have grown to manhood without walking beside water. In England and Wales alone, which is after all only a small plot of ground some 350 miles long by 250 miles across, there are two hundred and ten named rivers, besides innumerable brooks and streams. Rivers are a part of the English scene so intimate, so indistinguishable from the whole that there are few stretches of countryside in which you will not find a river flowing somewhere. The exile, when he dreams of home, dreams most often of fields and streams :—

> Oh shall I never be home again ?
> Meadows of England shining in the rain
> Spread wide your daisied lawns : your ramparts green
> With briar fortify, with blossom screen
> Till my far morning—and O streams that slow
> And pure and deep through plains and playlands go
> For me your love and all your kingcups store . . .

Who is there, born and bred in England, who has not somewhere in his mind a picture of such a meadow, framing a river bank, with a line of willows marking its course—willows whose intricate and denuded roots make such convenient clambering places for the boy with his bottle of minnows, the man with his pliant rod ? The fisherman is in fact almost as much a character-istic part of the English scene as the rivers, and many entrancing books have been written about fresh water fishing, but, because our space is limited, this must be a book primarily about the rivers themselves.

Rivers are in fact so integral a part of the English landscape that they tend to merge with the whole, and so become, like many other familiar things, almost forgotten. That flash of silver seen for a moment beneath the bridge as the cars roar along the by-pass, that broad flood over which Lon-

THE THAMES AT READING
Coloured aquatint by Joseph Farington, 1747-1821
From J. J. Boydell's *History of the River Thames*

GRETA BRIDGE, YORKSHIRE
Water colour by John Sell Cotman, 1805

doners pass twice daily as the trains carry them to and from their work : that clear swift-flowing stream at the foot of the fifty-acre, where the cattle drink in summer—these familiar waters, so often forgotten, are fluid history, bearing within their banks records of the pre-historic past, and also in a real and physical sense the shape of things to come. For as the writers of the best book on rivers written in these last twenty years so truly said: "Rivers have made England."

Her rivers have made England a nation by the facility of access to the sea (and from the sea inland) which they provide. This island of Great Britain, small as it is, has a tidal coast greater than that of any other nation in Europe. That coast is nearly four thousand miles in length, and a small vessel making landfall anywhere along it has hardly to feel her way coastwise for more than twenty miles in either direction before opening the mouth of a river up which she can penetrate into the mainland. The Thames and the Humber may be the only two estuaries on the East Coast of England, for example, having sufficient water to carry modern shipping far inland, but there are innumerable smaller rivers whose depth is amply sufficient to have floated the shallow-drafted craft of the early traders far into the heart of the country. In some cases their outlets to the sea may be guarded at low tide by narrow and often dangerous bars, but these could be crossed at high tide (as they still are crossed by countless yachts and smaller sailing craft) and there is nothing to show that the early seamen were at all likely to be daunted by such difficulties. Anyone who has sailed among the sand-banks and mud flats of the Thames estuary has only to imagine the difficulties which must have faced Caesar's galleys when they made their way up those then uncharted waters, to appreciate that his officers' knowledge of navigation must have been extensive.

Journeys which the undrained and roadless condition of the country made difficult in summer and impossible in winter, could be made simply and expeditiously by sea. By travelling down the nearest river to the sea; making a coastwise voyage (running the light craft ashore in a sheltered cove when the weather threatened), and striking inland again up a convenient river, the most difficult cross-country journeys could be avoided, and heavy cargoes, which the limited transport available made it impossible to carry far by road, could be taken from one end of the country to the other. Even to-day our coastwise traffic is considerable, and in early times it was the only possible means of conveying corn, coal and other material.

But if the rivers were valuable as a means of access to the sea, they were a thousand times more so as internal lines of communication. Rivers are, after all, but roads of water, and few countries have been so lavishly provided with these natural roads as England. If you could take a bird's-eye view of the country it would be seen as a sprawling creature with a great central vertebra from which innumerable rivers strike out east and west like veins, and even the smallest map will show you how conveniently distributed these

9

rivers are. They do almost everything which could be wanted of them as conveniently as if they had been designed for the purpose. The Thames, bearing all the produce of the southern counties to the sea (and thence north, south, east or west, wherever it was needed); the Trent, providing transport and communication up through the midlands to the northern counties; the Severn, linking the western counties with the sea—these great waterways alone served two-thirds of the country. What was lacking was provided by the innumerable possibilities of cross-country travel which resulted from the fortunate fact that the upper reaches of our eastward and westward running rivers are so often within a few miles of each other. How easy a haul it was from the upper reaches of the Thames to the Severn, or from the Fenland rivers to the Avon! The navigable rivers linked sea with sea, and north with south and so became the great civilising and socialising agents.

As the rivers formed so essential a part of the life of the country, it was inevitable that men should want to live as close to them as possible, and in fact the sites of almost all our principal towns were originally dictated by the topography of rivers. Many different factors influenced the selection of these sites.

In the first place, from time beyond memory the fordable places of rivers had been a cynosure of innumerable by-ways and footpaths from the surrounding countryside, and it was inevitable that villages and towns should spring up at such places. They were the natural centres of trade for the neighbourhood, and convenient places of assembly for local authority and government. Many of these towns still betray their origin in their names, such as Oxford, Chelmsford, Bishops Stortford, Guildford, Bradford and so on.

Then the great merchants and traders wanted to build their warehouses and stores beside the rivers at points where they were broad and deep enough to give space for wharves and moorings for the sea-going ships of their coastal trade. There is a town of this type at the mouth of every sizeable estuarial river (and of many which have long lost their importance, and even their access to the sea) and many of these also are named accordingly—Dartmouth, Exmouth, Falmouth, Portsmouth, Plymouth, Yarmouth and the rest.

The rivers were also for centuries the only known source of power and this was extensively employed by the millers, whose wooden wheels, though now fast falling derelict, were until the last century indispensable to agriculture. The watermill, with its millstream sluices and wooded islands, is still one of the most characteristic features of the English river. The communities which grew round and took their names from the mills were, however, principally agricultural and have in consequence not increased greatly with the passage of time, so that unless they were associated with other activities they have remained villages to this day.

1 Grand Union Canal
2 Trent and Mersey Canal
3 Weaver Navigation
4 Manchester Ship Canal
5 Rochdale Canal
6 Leeds and Liverpool Canal
7 Lancaster Canal
8 Aire and Calder Navigation
9 Ouse Navigation
10 Sheffield and South Yorkshire
    Navigation
11 Foss Dyke Canal
12 Newark Navigation
13 Shropshire Union Canals
14 Staffordshire and Worcestershire
    Canal
15 Coventry Canal
16 Worcester and Birmingham Ship
    Canal

17 Severn Navigation
18 Oxford Canal
19 Gloucester and Berkeley Ship
    Canal
20 Thames and Severn Canal
21 Wilts and Berks Canal
22 Thames Navigation
23 Kennet and Avon Navigation
24 Basingstoke Canal
25 Way and Arun Junction
26 Surrey Canal
27 Bridgewater and Taunton Canal
28 Grand Western Canal
29 Exeter Canal
30 Brecon and Abergavenny Canal
31 Glamorganshire Canal
32 Neath Canal
33 Tennant Canal
34 Swansea Canal

MAP SHOWING THE CHIEF RIVERS AND CANALS IN ENGLAND

Then again, religious communities, like the abbeys and priories whose occupants were the first systematic cultivators and husbandmen, settled beside rivers because their waters brought the alluvial deposits which made the richest soil; provided power for their mills; fish for their great ponds; and also, surely, because such surroundings were ideally suited for meditation and devotion? It cannot be entirely chance that of the hundreds of abbeys, priories and churches which give dignity and repose to our river banks, there is hardly one which has not been built in a position of great natural beauty. Of such are Tintern Abbey on the Wye, Buildwas on the Severn, Bolton on the Wharfe, Beaulieu, Medmenham, Christchurch; and the cathedrals—Ely, Canterbury, Salisbury, Lincoln, Durham, to name only a few that come to mind.

Finally there were the war-like communities of the great landowners, who built their castles, naturally enough, in positions which commanded the river approaches—and thus unconsciously provided future generations with some of the loveliest river views in England, among them Arundel Castle from the Arun; Windsor from the Thames; Conway; Rhuddlan; Chepstow; Haughton; Brancepeth; Ludlow and, to my mind the loveliest of them all, Warwick Castle from the Avon. There is something about this enduring admixture of moving water, trees, and weathered stone which is exactly right.

Possibly enough has been said to emphasise the importance of rivers in our national life, and little enough space has been left, in this brief introduction, to touch on another aspect of rivers as the makers of England. For her rivers have made England in a very real and physical sense. Their ceaseless scouring has worn down her hills, excavating the great winding valleys which are so typical a feature of our countryside; and the age-long process of planation has widened these valleys, producing the beautiful river terraces and the alluvial deposits whose richness is responsible for the lush riverside meadows which make this country such a green and pleasant land. Some of the most beautiful scenery in the country has been made by the meanders of rivers (a meander is the geologist's lovely name for a river's habit of straying from side to side of its valley in great opposing curves) fine examples of which can be seen in the valley of the Herefordshire Wye, on the Tees below Darlington, or on the Lune above Lancaster.

Even that scenery which does not depend for its beauty upon the presence of a river probably owes as much to river action in former ages. Geologists formerly believed that the configuration of a country was caused mainly by marine action, but subsequent researches have shown that the principal factor in shaping a country has always been subaerial action, principally that of meteoric water, which, falling as rain, becomes first a stream and then a river and in continually seeking a lower level, assisted by frost and by its own chemical constituents, breaks up rocks and mountains and carries away continents to the sea. The most spectacular consequences of denudation caused by rivers are probably the great gorges, as at Cheddar and Bristol and the

CHEPSTOW CASTLE ON THE WYE
Engraving from *Britannia Illustrata*, 1740

many smaller ones in the carboniferous limestone districts; but even more impressive, to my mind, are the great entrenched curves which rivers sometimes quarry a hundred feet and more below the level of the surrounding country. Magnificent examples of such curves can be seen on the Dart, near Dittisham, of which Lord Avebury, in his *Scenery of England*, laconically observes, "to understand such curves we must carry our minds back to the time when the river ran at a much higher level."

The larger English rivers are of great antiquity and have long established their regimens and settled down to spend the remainder of their lives flowing peacefully between their man-made embankments, but many of the more turbulent mountain streams are still comparatively youthful and have centuries of change yet to endure before their waters attain the quiet dignity of age.

Even the ancient rivers have not done with us yet. The Thames, for example, is estimated to carry some 450,000 tons of salt in solution annually to the sea, and forty years ago it was calculated that the rivers of England as a whole are lowering the general surface of the country by about one foot in every twelve thousand years.

But this is not a treatise on geology (if it were, much could be said on the importance of rivers, whose sunken deposits have yielded finds of incalculable value, to historians). Its object, if so slight a thing can be so dignified, is simply to serve as an introduction to a fascinating and inexhaustible subject.

13

*"There is not any Town or City, which hath
a navigable river at it, that is poore; nor
scarce any that are rich, which want a river
with the benefit of boats."* JOHN TAYLOR

SOMETHING has already been said about the convenience of our rivers
for transport, and it is possible that the writer's enthusiasm for moving
water may even have given the impression that the rivers were the
only means of water transport. In fact, of course, although this country has
probably the best distributed river system in the world for this purpose,
there were still some things which rivers could not do. They could not run
uphill, for example, nor could they traverse the valleys of other rivers.
Moreover, the navigation of the rivers was not uniformly good, and some
presented such difficulties, particularly in flood, that they were often unusable.
To solve these difficulties men have turned their thoughts to the construction of artificial waterways. It is believed that the Romans built some
military canals, and the Fossdyke, an ancient navigation linking the Trent
at Torksey with the Witham near Lincoln, has been attributed to them.
This canal, which is the oldest in England, was scoured out by Henry I,
and later was deepened to accommodate vessels of greater draft. The earliest
work, however, was devoted not to the actual construction of canals, but to
the improvement of river navigations, and from 1215 onwards innumerable
charters were granted for this purpose, and the work is still proceeding to
this day. But those interested in river navigation had to face bitter opposition
from rival interests before they accomplished their objects. The principal
opponents were the millers, who depended upon the head of water behind
the weirs to drive their water-wheels, and the riparian owners. This latter
class of person for long regarded the rivers as his own property, erected
weirs across them to assist in fish rearing, and diverted them across his
lands for irrigation. The right of free passage down other than tidal rivers
is disputed to this day, and there are still many stretches of river which are
known only to their owners, and to those with sufficient determination and
courage to brave the activities of water bailiffs.

None the less, the interests of navigation were obviously paramount, and
that they were generally so regarded is shown by a clause in Magna Carta
which states that, "all kidels [fish weirs] from henceforth shall be utterly
put down by Thames and Medway, and through all England, except
only by the sea coast." The real barriers to progress were the good old
English spirit of leave-well-alone and the fact that there was no authority
responsible for maintaining navigation on rivers. It was, in fact, not until
after 1600, when the population and trade of the country began to increase,
that serious attempts were made to improve the situation by granting Letters

THREE LOCKS AT STOKE HAMMOND, BUCKINGHAMSHIRE
Engraving from J. Hassell's *Tour of the Grand Junction Canal*, 1819

Patent to groups of undertakers (usually prominent local men) to control the navigation of individual rivers in the public interest.

Once a start had been made, progress was rapid, and in the seventy years between the Civil War and Defoe's tour in 1724-27 the mileage of navigable rivers increased from 685 to 1,160. During this period the general introduction of the pound lock brought about an immediate improvement in navigation on the larger rivers. The pound lock, such as we are accustomed to see on waterways to-day, was first used in this country on a canal built in 1566 by John Trew for the Corporation of Exeter in order to by-pass the weirs on the Exe, but did not come into general use until considerably later. Formerly the only method of improving the navigation of a river was by means of flashlocks or staunches. These were, in effect, movable obstructions which were used to hold back the water until a sufficient head had been raised, and were then suddenly withdrawn, the "flash" of water thus created carrying the vessels over the shallows below. Flashlocks varied in construction, but this description, written in 1826, of one on the Essex Stour, is typical of many :

"Two substantial posts, with a bottom cross cill, were fixed at a given distance apart, sufficient to permit a boat to pass easily between. Upon one of these posts was a beam, turning on its centre, and long enough to span the opening. When the staunch was used, the boatmen turned the beam across the opening and placed vertically in the stream a number of wooden planks, resting against the bottom cill and the swinging beam, thus forming

15

a weir, which raised the water in the stream about five feet high. The boards were then rapidly withdrawn, the swinging beam was turned back, and all the boats which had been collected above were carried by the flash over the shallows below. By repeating this operation at given intervals, the boats were enabled to proceed a distance of about 23 miles in two or three days."

It was impossible to proceed upstream against such a flash, and boats had, therefore, to be hauled up by means of a cable and winch. As can be imagined, this method of navigation was incredibly tedious, and yet it is not long since the last two flashlocks on the Thames (at Medley and Egton Weir, were removed, and staunches are still to be seen in the Fens and on parts of the Warwickshire Avon. Moreover, since the flashlock allowed a great quantity of water to run to waste every time it was opened, the bargemen were always at loggerheads with the millers, who naturally wanted to preserve a good head of water behind their weirs. Until the introduction of properly managed waterway boards or companies, the bargee's lot was, therefore, an unhappy one, consisting of a succession of arguments and delays at each lock before a flash was permitted, followed by frequent groundings in the shallows. The introduction of the pound lock brought immediate improvement in the navigation of rivers, and at the same time made possible the construction of canals, which towards the middle of the eighteenth century became imperative. The growth of the turnpike system had improved the roads considerably and brought about a great increase in passenger and light goods traffic, but the weight restrictions which had to be imposed to keep the roads in order made them unsuitable for the carriage of heavy goods. The beginnings of the industrial revolution found the country without the necessary means of distribution either for the coal and other materials which were needed for the factories, or for the finished goods. The consequence was an enormous increase in the development of river navigations, and the beginning of the canal age.

It is an interesting fact, and one seldom recorded, that it was inland waterways which first made possible the industrial revolution, and that a small stretch of canal between Worsley and Manchester is the cradle of England's modern industrial strength. This canal was finished in 1761 by the Duke of Bridgewater and his engineer, James Brindley, to carry coal from the Duke's pits at Worsley to Manchester. It was upon the cheap fuel thus provided that the prosperity of that town was founded. The canal was an immediate success and was later extended to Liverpool, a town to which in 1760 there was no carriage road. The Bridgewater Canal is still in use, and now incorporates one of the most remarkable examples of canal engineering in the country—the great swing aqueduct at Barton by which it is carried over the Manchester Ship Canal.

The success of the Bridgewater canal stimulated manufacturers and speculators throughout the country and the next thirty years saw a tremendous boom in canal construction. First of the great canals of this era was the

VIEW AT ROCKLIFFE ON THE TEES, YORKSHIRE
Water colour by John Sell Cotman, 1782-1842

MORNING ON THE RIVER
Coloured engraving by David Cox, 1783-1859

Trent and Mersey, then known as the Grand Trunk Canal, which was built by Brindley at the instigation of Josiah Wedgwood, to supply the potteries. The clay and flint for this industry had formerly to be brought from the south by sea, either to Chester or up the Severn, and carried thence by packhorse to the factories, the finished products being similarly distributed. The Grand Trunk connected the Trent at Wilden Ferry with the Mersey near Runcorn Gap, following a course between those two points best suited to the factories it was to serve, and it completely revolutionised the industry, not only on account of its convenience but also because the smoothness of water transport was ideally suited for the carriage of frangible goods and brought about a substantial reduction in breakages. Four years after it was completed, in 1781, John Wesley wrote :

"How is the whole face of this country changed in about twenty years ! Since the potteries were introduced, inhabitants have continually flowed in from every side. Hence the wilderness is literally become a fruitful field : houses, villages, towns, have sprung up; and the country is not more improved than the people."

The subsequent efforts of canal builders can be traced without difficulty on the map, since their natural desire, trade having for so long followed the courses of rivers, was to link rivers together by building canals over the intervening watersheds and so provide a through route from one side of the country to the other. From the Grand Trunk was built the Staffordshire and Worcestershire Canal, which linked both the Trent and Mersey with the Severn at Stourport; and the Oxford and Coventry canals, which joined the same rivers with the Thames at Oxford. So the web grew.

The next threads were woven across the backbone of England, by the Leeds and Liverpool Canal, which linked the Mersey with the Aire and Calder Navigations of Yorkshire, and the Huddersfield Canal, linking Manchester with the Calder on a more southerly line. Lastly, after the turn of the century, the southern links were added by two canals built to connect the Bristol Avon with the Thames, the Kennet and Avon at Reading and the Wilts and Berks at Abingdon; and a third, the Thames and Severn, to provide a direct link between these two great rivers. The final link in this great chain of inland waterways was joined in 1805, when the Grand Junction Canal was built to link the Thames near London with the Grand Trunk, thus providing a through route up the heart of England. North, South, East and West the great waterways were now complete, and in between them smaller canals were added by degrees until there was hardly an industry in England which could not send its products to any part of the country by waterway. Curiously enough, the heart of this great network of waterways is not, as in the case of road and rail transport, London, but Birmingham, a fact principally responsible for the initial prosperity of that town.

The cutting of all these canals was a great engineering undertaking, and was not carried out without blood and sweat. The navvies (or navigators as the men working on canals were called) invaded the countryside in such numbers that English village life, which had remained undisturbed for centuries, was completely disrupted. The wages offered also attracted so many agricultural labourers to the camps that a Bill had to be introduced in 1793 to prohibit work on the construction of canals during harvest time, lest there should be insufficient men available to gather the crops. Incidents such as this described in a paragraph from the *Exeter Flying Post* were all too common :

"On Wednesday last an inquest was held on the body of a man named Helps, who was shot dead by Mr. Chave. The jury, after the examination of a number of witnesses, returned a verdict of "Justifiable Homicide." The deceased, it seems, was one of the men employed in excavating the Grand Western Canal, a party of whom were engaged in an affray with some of the villagers, when the unfortunate man met his death."

And the impact of advertisements such as this (also from the *Exeter Flying Post* in 1810) on village life, can well be imagined :

"*Wanted*, Two or Three Hundred Good Workmen on the Worcester and Birmingham Canal, where liberal prices will be given to Agg Masters, and good wages to workmen that are steady and deserving encouragement."

It is curious that the only other occasions when similar invasions of the countryside have taken place have each been connected with transport; during the last century when the railways were built, and during the present war when the great airfields were under construction.

The problems encountered in constructing the canals also brought into being a new professional class, the civil engineers. Before the canals were built, the modern science of roadmaking was almost unknown, the railways were still undreamt of, and there was in consequence no necessity for such a class. Many great names were made from the canals—Telford, Brindley, Smeaton, the Rennies, Jessop, Mylne, Whitworth, Cubitt—men who, working in the days before the Ordnance Survey, when the land was almost unknown, worked carefully over the ground, took correct levels, and knew enough of geology to avoid the worst disasters. For disasters there were, and more than one projected canal had to be abandoned and the shareholders' money lost, for want of an accurate survey of the proposed route.

Anyone who, as a boy, has made channels among mud or sand, can imagine something of the difficulties which faced these men in making navigable waterways, seventy or a hundred miles in length, up hill and down dale, across almost unknown country. Tunnels had to be built, bridges to carry roads over the canals, and aqueducts to carry the canals themselves over rivers and valleys. The aqueduct which was built by Telford to carry the Ellesmere Canal (now the Shropshire Union) over the valley of the Dee (to name only one example) is over a thousand feet long. To overcome sudden rises in level ingenious alternatives to locks were invented, such as the inclined plane and the canal lift.

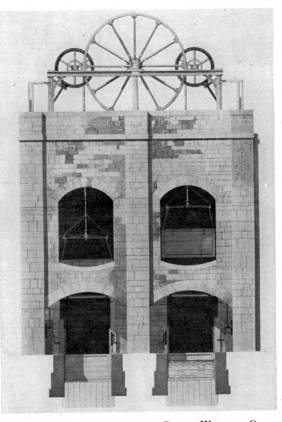

A PERPENDICULAR LIFT ON THE GRAND WESTERN CANAL
Engraving by S. Bellin after a drawing by J. Green, 1836

The inclined plane was a long slope between two levels of canal, laid with rails. The barges were either fitted with wheels which ran on the rails, being raised or lowered as required; or were floated into caissons, which were similarly raised or lowered : steam or hydraulic power was then used to raise the barge from one level to another. The lift provided a vertical rise on the principle of the counter-balance. At one time there were a number of these lifts and planes in England, the remains of which can still be traced by the curious, but there are no planes now in use, and only one lift—at Anderton, connecting the Weaver Navigation with the Trent and Mersey (formerly the Grand Trunk) Canal.

Such were the canals, seemingly the beginning of a great and prosperous undertaking, but though their early history was fortunate enough their subsequent record is a gloomy one of gradual decline and fall. The trade

A VIEW OF THE DUKE OF BRIDGEWATER'S AQUEDUCT OVER THE RIVER MERSEY
Engraving from the *Gentleman's Magazine*, 1766

was there, the transport facilities were adequate, if not exceptional, and the possibilities of economical transport must have appeared immense, but with rare exceptions their proprietors made insufficient effort to overcome the competition of the railways. Those canals constructed between 1760 and 1790 were almost uniformly successful. They were built very cheaply and through areas which were ready for industrial development, and they therefore immediately attracted a large trade. The Duke of Bridgewater's canal, for example, cost £220,000 to construct, but by 1792 was bringing in a revenue of £80,000 per annum from freight: the Oxford Canal, 91 miles in length, completed in 1789, by 1820 was paying 32 per cent. dividends: the £100 shares of the little Loughborough Navigation stood in 1824 at £4,600. On the other hand, those which were built during the Napoleonic wars suffered from the high prices of labour and materials, which vitiated the estimates (there was an increase of 90 per cent. in wholesale prices between 1790 and 1810), and from the over-optimism of canal speculators. The Kennet and Avon, for example, for which £420,000 was considered sufficient capital, eventually cost over a million pounds to construct; and between 1811 and 1814 eleven miles of the Grand Western, and those without any locks and with only one short tunnel, cost £244,000, whereas twenty years earlier a smaller sum had been thought sufficient to construct the entire length of forty-six miles, including many locks. Moreover, many of these later canals were built on a speculative basis through agricultural areas, in the hope of creating sufficient trade to make them profitable. In many such cases the only profitable period for the companies was while they were carrying the materials to build the railways which finally extinguished them.

By 1820, most of the present canal system, and many navigations now derelict, had been built. The four years that followed, until the great slump of 1825 finally extinguished such dreams, were the halcyon period of great canal projects. During these years speculators and engineers, followed enthusiastically by the general public, put their thoughts above the barge canals and planned waterways which could bring ships across the land. The completion in 1822, after many vicissitudes, of the great state-owned Caledonian Canal linking the east and west coasts of Scotland, gave stimulus and encouragement to these projects, among which were the English and Bristol Channels Ship Canal, the London and Portsmouth Ship Canal and the Manchester and Dee Ship Canal. These schemes were beginning to take practical shape and many millions of capital were talked of, when the great slump brought all such speculations to an end. When the economic situation again allowed such schemes to be considered the day of canals was over. Only the Gloucester and Berkeley, the Exeter, and the Norwich and Lowestoft ship canals indicate what might have been if the invasion of railways had been postponed.

Of this last named canal, William Cole, the Clerk of Works, wrote the following remarkable lines :

Hail ! Norwich, hail ! this memorable day,
Raise the loud peal—your waving flags display !
All classes now unite with just applause,
And greet the Champions of your City's cause :
Soon shall we see your stately vessels ride,
With canvas spreading to the swelling tide,
(As their gay streamers with the breezes sport)
And land their cargoes in the wished-for Port ;
Commerce will o'er your ancient city spread,
And the mechanic raise his languid head ;
Your manufactories revive again,
Whilst careful farmers load your fleets with grain ;
And wealthy merchants too their aid impart,
Freighting their produce to some distant mart.

But the construction of these canals (though the Manchester Ship Canal remained to be built) was really the end of the great canal era. Railway competition soon became serious. A few canal companies started to improve their services, and nearly all made drastic cuts in their charges, thus further reducing their revenues, but modernisation, which would have been the only answer, was made impossible by the fact that the capital necessary was now flowing to their competitors. Many canal companies sold themselves to the railways almost immediately, seventeen companies being thus swallowed up in the year 1846 alone. Some founded railways on their own account, like the Trent and Mersey, which promoted the North Staffordshire Railway :

upon the beds of others, railways were made, as in the case of the Croydon and the Glastonbury Canals. The remainder kept up a losing fight, hung on and waited for better times. On most of the independent navigations which thus continued the tonnage carried did not greatly decrease, but the receipts were much lower. On the Basingstoke Canal, for example, the receipts per ton carried in 1813 were 4s. 3d., and by 1865 they had been reduced to 1s. 0d., the quantity carried being approximately the same.

In all, about one-third of the total waterway mileage in the country was brought under railway control. If each canal be considered separately, it is probable that it fared little worse than it would have done had it remained in independent hands, but if the waterway system be considered as a whole, it will be seen that railway acquisition effectually prevented large-scale amalgamation and modernisation, since many of the vital links in possible through routes were railway owned. Another factor was the comparatively low earning power of the canals, which prevented them from raising capital. And so throughout the 19th century more and more canals were closed and river navigations fell derelict. Canals which simply ceased to function for lack of revenue were allowed to dry up, and their sunken course can still be traced in many parts of the country, such as the Wey and Arun Junction Canal between Shalford (Wey) and Newbridge (Arun), or the Portsmouth and Arundel Canal between Ford (Arun) and Chichester Harbour. The river navigations fared even worse, for as they fell into neglect the timbers of the disused locks and staunches perished for want of attention, the brick and stone work crumbled and decayed and the rotting remains collapsed into the river beds, effectually preventing navigation even for the smallest craft. It seemed that the waterways were doomed, and that the rivers which had been for so many centuries the life blood of the country would cease to be living highways and become simply isolated stretches of water between obstructions.

But towards the end of the century, public opinion began to swing towards the canals. Railways were prevented by legislation from buying further canals, or from charging unreasonable rates on those they already owned, and the completion of the great Manchester Ship Canal in 1894 once more brought inland navigation into the limelight. Soon after the turn of the century, a Royal Commission was established to consider the whole question of waterways. This Commission did some excellent work, and its recommendations were admirable, but as with so many similar Reports, nothing was done. Its members proposed that the waterways should be re-organised as a whole, based on the main lines of the great "cross"—the waterways linking the Midlands with the Thames, the Humber, the Mersey and the Severn. A subsequent Royal Commission on transport in 1930 made similar recommendations. The greatest single factor in the failure of the canals to compete with the railways has always been their lack of co-ordination. Not only were different sections of all through routes controlled by competing companies (on the three routes between London and Liverpool,

ETRURIA : THE POTTERIES
Oil painting by Hesketh Hubbard

for instance, there were until 1894 twenty-eight different companies), but the widths of the locks on each section varied, as did also the widths and depths of the canals themselves.

Meanwhile, what of the waterways to-day? The picture is not all gloom, for the past twenty years have seen a certain amount of progress, most of it on rivers rather than canals, recent research and experiment on land drainage and flood control having revived interest in the river navigations. Among many fine works those on the Nene and the Trent may be quoted as typical examples of modern river navigations. The Nene has been re-locked throughout in the last twelve years, and a modern type of lock, having special steel gates at the lower end to pass flood water, has been fitted. What lovely names some of these locks have! Alwalton, Waternewton, Wansford, Yarwell, Cotterstock, Barnwell, Lilford, Wadenhoe, Islip, Denford. The tidal lock on this navigation, which might so easily have been called Nene Navigation No. 1 has by the good sense of the proprietors been left with its old name of "Dog-in-a-Doublet." The navigation being now completed, there is regular traffic on the upper part of this river, and barges from London pass to Peterborough. The Trent also has been re-locked and the navigation improved from Shardlow, near Derby, to the Humber. These are fine modern locks which can pass a train of four barges carrying six hundred tons of cargo in one operation and, owing to the greater width and depth of the navigation, comparatively high speeds can be permitted, so that a train of barges can steam from Hull to Nottingham in eighteen hours. The Trent can float quite sizeable vessels, and it is a fine sight to see a large tug with her train of great steel barges steaming through the countryside sixty or seventy miles from the sea.

Another fine modern navigation is the Aire and Calder, which both serves Yorkshire and links the Humber with the Mersey. Leeds, which is served by this navigation, receives no less than one-third of its industrial and domestic coal supplies by water. This navigation, like the Trent, is sufficiently enterprising to maintain a motor transport fleet, and is also famous for its compartment boats or "Tom Puddings." These curious craft are simply rectangular steel tanks, designed so that they can be hauled out of the water on trolleys and taken by rail to the collieries for loading, after which they are lowered into the water and coupled up behind a tug, like so many railway wagons. A single tug can pull a train of nineteen of these boats, carrying some seven to eight hundred tons of coal, and the locks on the lower portion of the navigation are large enough to accommodate an entire train at a single operation. This navigation is also probably unique in that it possesses its own port of Goole, on the Humber.

Extensive modernisation has been carried out on the routes owned by the Grand Union Canal Company—the first great amalgamation of canal companies, which in 1929 took over the Grand Junction, Leicestershire and Northamptonshire Union, Warwick and Birmingham, Warwick and Napton, Grand Union, Regent's and Hertford Union Canals, and in 1932 added the Loughborough Navigation, the Erewash Canal and the Leicester Navigation. This company now controls three hundred miles of navigable waterways over which, with Government assistance, standardisation has been largely completed. To prevent delays an elaborate system of craft control has been devised, as a result of which barges can now travel from Birmingham to London in fifty hours, and the company has carried inland navigation to its logical conclusion by founding a shipping line to carry goods direct from its own docks to all parts of the world.

Canal companies and navigations have been, not unnaturally, chary of imparting information about their war-time activities, but from observation during extensive travelling about the country in the past two years, it is obvious that a very large burden of traffic has been carried, and it is possible that a new era of prosperity has dawned for the waterways. This increasing traffic has brought not only new life, but renewed beauty to these waterways. Canals have a charm which is all their own, and it is a charm which is curiously enhanced by the presence of traffic. A highway looks nowadays very much the worse for its passengers, but a canal is never so much itself as when the gaily coloured barges are chugging along it.

FLATFORD MILL ON THE RIVER STOUR
Oil painting by John Constable, 1776-1837

III

"I love discourse of rivers."
IZAAC WALTON

AND now, having cleared our ground, we come at last to the roots of the matter—what are these rivers which have made England? After talking so long at large, it is perhaps unfortunate that the particular cannot be avoided, for individual rivers are at once the most entrancing and the most perplexing things to write about—and what a deal has already been written about them! From the Nailborne streams of Kent to the great waterways of the Severn, Thames and Trent there is hardly a river or stream so small that someone has not had something to say on the subject, and from the journals of local topographical societies to the vast, elaborately bound and often painfully illustrated collections of the last century, so much has been written that no one man can keep pace with it—and how dull it all is! With rare exceptions, such as *Rivers of the South* by A. B. Austin,

25

which is made memorable both by the understanding and insight of its text and the superb photographs with which it is illustrated, the innumerable topographical and historical accounts of rivers are of a positively astounding prolixity and dullness. There may be persons who enjoy these tedious collections of familiar facts, who like to know that the Lady Blanche was immured for seven years in the castle which you can just see if you climb that hill four miles from the river, or that the old Norman church six miles to the east has some interesting brasses; but your true lover of rivers is not among them. I speak feelingly on this subject, for my love of rivers has driven me at one time and another during the past twenty years to read almost everything which has been written about them, and it is only after such a course of study that one appreciates the true inwardness of Bacon's dictum that, "reading maketh a full man."

Rivers are not to be known from books. If you really want to learn anything about a river, you must go and look at it, follow its course by walking along its banks, or better still, by travelling down it in a canoe or whatever kind of craft you can buy or borrow. Rivers are living things and to know them intimately you must live with them, go with them on their voyaging and see the places they visit, and best of all these places are those which can only be reached by water, which only the fisherman and the canoer ever see. Little wooded islands in midstream; shingly beaches beneath overhanging banks; backwaters, or mortlakes, made by the river cutting across the head of one of its great meanders—in places such as these it is possible to travel backwards in time with the river, living the life it has lived for centuries, unknown even to the generations of children playing on its banks. For in their upper reaches our rivers often wander for as much as fifteen or twenty miles without a bridge or even a ford, and though village footpaths sometimes follow one bank for a few miles, there is always a far bank, inaccessible, remote, which the traveller by water can claim for his own.

Moreover, he who sets out to rediscover England in this way will not travel alone, for Englishmen have recently begun to use their rivers as they should be used, though this time not for commerce but for pleasure. In the years before the war wherever you wandered beside rivers, in the Welsh mountains, or among the moors and fells of the North, before long you would come across a small party of adventurers hauling their canoes over a weir, or setting up their tents on the bank. The late Lord Baden Powell was one of the first to practise this new sport, and the books describing his tours were among the first of a new kind of river book which has become popular in the past twenty years, though there are as yet very few of them. But most of these books also are unhappily almost as dull as that other kind referred to above, for their authors have felt themselves obliged to fill out their pages with the familiar guide-book information. A notable exception is Mr. William Bliss's *Rapid Rivers*, which is one of those rare books on specialist subjects, like *Racundra's First Cruise*, or Mr. S. C. H. Davis's fine book on motor

WATERMILL, CUMBERLAND
Water colour by Peter de Wint, 1784-1849

racing, which are books in their own right, and which anyone can read with pleasure and profit even though he knows nothing of the subject. For Mr. Bliss is above guide books and he writes as a true river man should, of the rivers themselves and of the living people he met on their banks.

This brief survey of rivers does not attempt to reproduce information which can be obtained in greater detail elsewhere, nor does it pretend to be exhaustive. First-hand information is the only kind that is really valuable where rivers are concerned, and I propose, therefore, to write principally of the rivers that I have known. If your own favourite stream is not mentioned, or is dismissed with only a passing reference, do not think that it has been ignored. Far from it, there is no English river or stream however small, that is not worthy of mention, and my only reason will have been that I did not feel qualified to write about it.

Anyone writing of the English rivers must inevitably come first to consider the three great waterways, Severn, Thames and Trent. None of them is really very much as rivers go—the longest of them, in fact, is little more than two hundred miles—but they are the biggest we have and what they lack in size is more than compensated for by other qualities. Equally obviously, the first of these three rivers to be considered must be the Thames, father of rivers, about which sufficient must already have been written to fill a fair-sized library.

The Thames is probably the oldest English river. It has been flowing in something like its present course from time immemorial (pre-Roman fortifications at Dorchester show that the river was running in the same course and at the same level two thousand years ago) and geologists tell us that aeons before recorded time it existed as a tributary of the Rhine or some other great river running westward from that continent of which England was then a part. It is, undoubtedly, one of the oldest of all the rivers existing in the world as we know it to-day, and it is, of course, only right that the doyen of English rivers should be of such a respectable antiquity. Yet I must confess to something of a prejudice against the Thames, which is somehow altogether too orderly, regimented and sedate for it ever to become one of my favourites. It has been flowing for so many centuries that it has long established its regimen, levelled out the inequalities of strata between its source and the sea, and carved out for itself a bed whose fall is throughout gradual, unarduous and uneventful. Its battle with the rocks is so long forgotten that there is hardly a ripple left in its whole course other than those made by weirs and locks and other works of men. The Thames is, in fact, so old that one almost forgets it ever had a history and imagines that it has always been exactly as it is to-day, timeless and eternal.

This air of immutability is, no doubt, a thing so essentially English that it must be accepted as one aspect of the country and its rivers. But it is not the only aspect, though it is, perhaps unfortunately, the one with which

OLD BATTERSEA BRIDGE, THE THAMES
Oil painting by Walter Greaves, 1846-1931

foreigners are most familiar. This very air of placid calm which other nations find so infuriating has only been made possible by the achievements of that other aspect of the English temperament which drove men down her rivers to the sea and so over half the world, adventuring, exploring and conquering. It is because I believe profoundly that this spirit is still alive, and that the English have by no means finished with the world, that the rivers I love are the small rapid streams which come swashbuckling down mountain sides, jostling rocks out of their way, and having a high time about their business with the world.

Yet when all this is said, and even when it is admitted that the Thames is at times a little dull, what a noble river it is ! Though no longer "a mile across at Kew," it is still an impressive body of water in its majestic passage through London, and it has been a part of history since the first Englishman looked out from his cave in the chalk cliffs at the swift, gravel-shored stream pouring through its deep gorge. In those days it must have been an impressive sight—we know, for example, that in some past time it required a valley floor ten miles in breadth—and it was still swift and clear, streaming through ravines and gorges which it has long levelled out. Where London now stands, for example, the river ran through a great ravine, the bottom of which has been estimated to be at Charing Cross eighty feet and more below the present surface of the river.

The Thames was formerly navigable as far as Lechlade for small vessels. An Act of 1751 recites that the Thames had been navigable "from time immemorial" from the City of London to the village of Burcot in Oxfordshire, and from Oxford to Lechlade, and that the stretch between had been made navigable in 1624. Such considerable use was made of the navigation that it was estimated that at one time no less than twenty thousand men were employed as bargemen or lightermen. Even more remarkable, however, particularly in view of its complete abandonment in this century, was the use of the Thames as the "silent highway" of London. Until the time of the Stuarts the river was the principal means of transport for journeys of any distance, both for the upper and lower classes, and every family of consequence upon its banks maintained its private barge just as later its coach, or to-day its car. Wherries, tilt boats and barges plied their trade in such numbers that in 1655 it was found necessary to introduce an Act regulating their charges in order to prevent the frequent brawls which arose. The fare to Gravesend, for example, was 2d., to Chertsey 1s. 4d., and to Windsor 10s.

It is clear from contemporary accounts that the river was an important and vital part of the life of the city, and one has only to remember the great water pageants; the royal barges and processions; the yacht races, and the fairs on the ice; to read Pepys's Diary, or remember Johnson and Boswell taking a boat to Greenwich for the day—landing at the Old Swan and walking to Billingsgate to avoid the heavy rapids at London Bridge—to appreciate how intimately the river was bound up with the normal life of the Londoner. No other English river has ever had such a considerable passenger traffic, nor has any comparable river so little to-day, when as Mr. A. P. Herbert in his eloquent *No Boats on the River*, has so justly pointed out, there is no point in inner London at which a craft can be moored. No doubt the Port of London Authority knows its own business, but it has always seemed to me a sad thing that the Londoner should have to travel so far afield to use his own river, and I never see the stretches between Battersea and Westminster without reflecting how pleasant it would be if the citizen of London could stroll down to their banks of a summer evening and spend his leisure sailing or rowing among the historic buildings of this ancient city. Above Teddington Lock the work of the Thames Conservancy has made the river accessible and convenient for all to use, but buses or trains are necessary to reach this part of the river from London, and a crowded journey robs the trip of half its pleasure.

The beauty of the Thames has been so much praised, and is so familiar, that it should hardly be necessary to say much here about it. Scenes like Cliveden Woods, the stretches where the river pierces the Chilterns, the

ENTRANCE TO MAIDSTONE, ON THE MEDWAY
Water colour by E. T. Holding, 1924

valley above Richmond, are all as familiar as Westminster Abbey, and deservedly, for the typical Thames-side scene with its meadows and woods is a part of the English heritage. The particular beauty of the Thames is her wide valleys, and the sometimes extraordinary effect of consummate artistry which the final result of her meanderings has achieved. The river curves exactly as it should to extract the last ounce of beauty from the landscape, and the trees often seem as though they had been deliberately planted to enhance the effect. The Thames meanders are, of course, often on so grand a scale that they have to be seen from the air to be appreciated fully, but the reach above Richmond, which can be seen from Richmond Hill, is justly famous.

The Thames is fortunate also in her tributaries, of which she has more, I believe, than any other English river. With the single exception of the Medway, which is something of a changeling, they are a pleasant brood of friendly and lovable little rivers. Windrush, Evenlode, Cherwell, Wey, Mole, Darent, Thame, Loddon (to name only a few), they are lovely and quiet in their flowing, and they water some of England's pleasantest pasture lands. But with the possible exceptions of the Wey, which was once a navigation of some importance, and the Lea which still carries a considerable traffic, they are none of them of any great importance on their own account.

The Medway, on the other hand, always has been and still is an important and prosperous navigation. It is only technically a tributary of the Thames, for though it enters the estuary before the coast line curves back to the sea, it is really a Kentish river. It has long been navigable for twenty or more miles inland, and before the roads were made, was the great highway carrying the produce of Kent to London. Its twin ports of Chatham and Rochester are known to seamen the world over as a naval base, and as the home of the sailing barges. These lovely vessels (which with their crew of two are probably among the most efficient and economical work vessels ever evolved) can still be seen moored in tiers in the Pool, seeming with their top-masts housed and their great sprit-sails brailed up, for all the world like swans asleep on the water. It is characteristic of the Thames and its family that these few miles of Medway water should be the home of two of man's loveliest creations —these sailing barges and the silver flying boats higher up the river. The old and the new in perfect conjunction, each consummately designed to fulfil its own function and, therefore, inevitably a thing of beauty.

But, for all the loveliness of Thames and its tributaries, to me it is only really interesting below London Bridge, when it becomes once again a living river going about its business as a river should. The whole duty of rivers is to carry men to the sea, and few rivers have done more of this than the Thames, which houses on its banks, many miles from the sea, the greatest general cargo port in the world, and has for centuries brought the ships of all nations up river to the Pool.

But this fascination, this endless and inexhaustible delight of London river, is not really riverine at all. The spell which holds small boys enthralled on bridges gazing at the ships, which makes the whole dock area with its irritating walls over which the uninitiated can see so little, an enchanted and bewitching place, is not the same spell which holds us as we watch a young river tumbling among its rocks. It is the magic of the sea, of "The Spanish sailors with bearded lips, and the beauty and mystery of the ships." And so though no-one, and more especially a Londoner, can ever quite escape from the lure of the Thames, when I think of English rivers I think first of other streams more to my liking, of the Wye, the Derwent, the Avon and the Dee—or the Severn.

For the Severn is a river after my own heart. It is all things that a river should be, and in its passage from the Welsh mountains to the sea, the traveller can watch unfold a changing pageant of riverhood, from its first beginnings as a mountain stream, through its gradual broadening and deepening into a full-grown river, until finally it becomes the great and dangerous waterway of its lower reaches. And it is, except for the scene of not unpicturesque dereliction at Ironbridge, almost entirely unspoilt.

The Severn rises in wild, desolate country at the foot of Plinlimmon, an area which fathers four of our loveliest rivers, for the Wye and the Rheidol both spring from the same source, and the Dee rises only some twenty or thirty miles to the north. Thereafter it travels swiftly, for it is never really sluggish, through a hundred and eighty miles of country, some of which is as lovely as any in England, none of which is marred by industry and all of which is

DEMONSTRATION OF THE THEORY OF NAVIGABLE CANALS
Coloured engraving by J. Pass, 1800

THE FIRST BRIDGE AT PADDINGTON ON THE GRAND JUNCTION CANAL
An Accommodation Barge going down the Canal to Uxbridge
Coloured aquatint published in 1801

pleasant. It is without question the best river run in England, for from Llanidloes, only some fifteen miles from its source, to the first lock at Lincombe, a matter of over a hundred miles, there are no locks and very few weirs. It is also the loveliest journey that any man could hope to make, for in these hundred miles the river passes by mountain and meadow, moorland and fell, by every kind of habitation from cottages to towns, and glances in passing at every changing aspect of the English scene. The lovely winding valleys below the Breidens or Wenlock Edge and the deep and quiet stretch through the Wyre Forest are as lovely as any in England, and even when the river comes to a town, its charm is increased rather than diminished. For the Severn towns are none of them large enough to have outgrown their river, and all of them have in generous measure that quiet and picturesque beauty which seems especially to belong to an historic riverside town. Shrewsbury, Worcester, Tewkesbury, Gloucester—what river could be more fortunate in its towns? Gloucester may be perhaps not so fortunate in its river as the river in its town, for only the freakish Severn tide, with its treacherous bore has prevented it from becoming one of the greatest English ports. This bore, a three-foot wall of water which sweeps up the river bed with every incoming tide, made it necessary for a ship canal to be built in order to by-pass the dangerous lower reaches of the river.

Through all these changing scenes the river bears you on its swift flood with the minimum of difficulty and yet with just sufficient variety of rapid and weir for you to feel when you have done that you have accomplished a journey worth making, and learnt some of the many things that a river can teach you.

We are told that in earliest times the Severn was navigable for barges as far as Pool Quay, over a hundred and fifty miles from the sea. Little trace of this navigation now remains on the upper reaches but that it formerly existed is well authenticated, as for example, by a Statute of Henry VI's which was passed in consequence of certain "Welshmen and other ill-disposed persons who used to assemble in manner of war and stop trows, boats and floats or drags on the way to Bristol, Gloucester and other places, and hew in pieces their craft and beat their sailors, with intent to force them to hire boats from the said Welshmen for great sums of money." A later Act, dealing with the same lamentable practice, contains the memorable statement that "time out of mind merchants and others have used the Severn without interruption, trouble, vexation, let or disturbance . . . and without anything therefore paying or giving." This ancient right of free navigation still exists between Pool Quay and Stourport, at which town the modern navigation commences, and anyone is free to put a boat on the river between these two places and travel as he will. Would that it were true of all rivers !

Below Stourport the Severn is under the jurisdiction of the Severn Commissioners, but it is still a remarkably inexpensive river to use, the lockage fee being only threepence for small craft. I remember once passing from the Avon into the Severn at Tewkesbury and being immediately confronted with the enormous barrier of the Upper Lode Lock (one of the largest inland locks in the country) and the shame I felt when the lock-keeper with great courtesy insisted on opening it for me, and refused to take more than the statutory threepence. I shudder to think how many hundreds of thousands of gallons that operation used, and all for a twelve-foot canoe—and three-pence !

Something has already been said about the third of our great rivers, the Trent, and when that little is said, there is very little left to say. For the Trent is somehow an unlovable and disillusioned sort of river. I do not quite know why this should be, for it has many stretches which are pleasant and some which have an attraction all their own, such as the long meandering passage through Cannock Chase. But, taken as a whole, the river is too brisk, bleak and business-like to be bothered with casual visitors, and it is notable that for all its seeming suitability, few pleasure craft use its waters. This may, perhaps, be because the river is too fast, and certainly it has a most purposeful current, being in midstream too much for even the most practised swimmer, as I know from experience; but I think the real reason is that it does not welcome anyone who is not bringing grist to its mills. Its wide, undeviating waters, pouring relentlessly down to the sea through mile upon mile of unchanging, level and unprofitable-looking pasture land, were designed for barges and tugs, for business and not for pleasure. The barge trains can look very impressive at times, and the locks and weirs are fine examples of modern rivercraft, and I take off my hat to the Trent Navigation Company for doing a fine job of work—and myself to another river.

Logic may demand that anyone writing of English rivers should treat first of her great waterways, but when that is done, it becomes almost impossible to be systematic, for the rivers defy classification. Many attempts have been made by different writers to divide the rivers into watertight compartments—Welsh rivers, Devon rivers, East Coast rivers, West Coast rivers, and so on—but they insist on overflowing from one compartment into another. For they are not conveniently grouped for this sort of thing, nor do they obey any order in their flowing. Let us, therefore, for want of a better plan, write of the rivers as they come to mind, and if some sort of order emerges it will be that of natural preference, which is the best of all orders.

First, then, among the lesser rivers, if not among all rivers, is surely the Warwickshire Avon, the loveliest and most typically English of all our rivers. Though there are three Avons—a Hampshire one flows from near Devizes to the English Channel at Christchurch, and a Somersetshire one from the Cotswolds to the Bristol Channel at Avonmouth—this Warwickshire Avon, which rises near Naseby and follows a meandering course through sixty

DROPGATE ON THE SEVERN
Water colour by John Sell Cotman, 1782-1842

miles of England's loveliest meadows to join the Severn at Tewkesbury, has long appropriated the name to itself. A stranger who wanted to see this country at her best could hardly do better than follow its course, for there is not a mile which does not present something either of interest or beauty, and hardly a yard which the passage of time has spoiled. Such towns as are to be found on its banks are themselves as ancient and peaceful as the river, and its only contact with industry is still, as it has been for a thousand years, as a motive power for the mills.

The land which the Avon waters is wholly given over to agriculture. It is a country of meadow-lands and orchards, of somnolent villages and drowsy towns, and change and development seem to have passed it by. Such change as it has undergone has only made it the quieter, for it was once a prosperous navigation to Stratford, capable of bearing vessels up to fifty tons. But the navigation above Pershore (which is, or was until before the war, still visited twice a week by a motor vessel bringing grain to the mill) has long been derelict. The locks have crumbled and decayed and their stones, falling into the river, have made little rapids and waterfalls, and quiet pools which are the haunt of anglers. It is typical of the Avon that even the navigation below Pershore still makes use of so ancient a device as a staunch to provide sufficient depth of water for the boats going up to the mill.

The whole course of the Avon is studded with mills, many of which are still in use, including that one at Guy's Cliff which is reputed to have been turning for over nine hundred years, and on the upper reaches when the water is low, you can watch its level change as it has done for centuries when the millers open and close their sluices. It is this plenitude of mills which gives the Avon its unhurried and sometimes even sluggish gait, for if it were left to itself, it would be quite a brisk little river, as can be seen from the pleasant little rapids which it makes when it gets for a moment beyond the influence of a weir. But the Avon was never intended to be a swift stream and it is better as it is, straying peacefully through the meadows of Stratford and the pleasant vale of Evesham, or winding slowly and reposefully below Bredon, a river as English and imperturbable as the great poet with whose name it will always be associated.

If the Avon is the most peaceful of English rivers, the Wye is probably the most magnificent. So much has been written already about the Wye valley that it is difficult, even supposing it were necessary, to say anything which has not been said before, and said better, by those who earlier saw its lovely wooded valleys and limestone gorges. But no account of our rivers could be complete without due praise having been given to the most picturesque of them all. For in the whole of its hundred and thirty miles from Plinlimmon to the Severn estuary, the Wye is never commonplace for a mile. Its courses take it far from industry and the works of man through country which has preserved its natural beauty intact, and it is remarkable among rivers in that its first waters are not its fastest, some of its wildest, rockiest

BEDDGELERT BRIDGE, WALES
Water colour by Cornelius Varley, 1805

and most turbulent reaches occurring after it has become a full-grown river. For it is a deep and rapid flood, bearing the traveller, in high water, for a hundred miles without let or hindrance—there are no locks anywhere on the Wye, which has not been navigable these hundred years and more, though we are told that small barges could formerly travel up river as far as Hay Bridge.

The Wye has for some reason acquired a reputation as a dangerous river, which is quite undeserved, for though there are many rapids, few of them present difficulty to anyone with his wits about him and even the famous Monnington Falls and Symond's Yat, though heavy and turbulent, are deep and consequently not dangerous to a good craft and a stout heart. Monnington Falls in particular need not even be attempted, for there is usually a perfectly safe channel to the right which avoids the fall.

The Wye has many beauties, the forty miles below Ross in particular making it necessary to abandon superlatives as inadequate, but her crowning glory is her trees. For trees are everywhere, crowding down to her banks among the gorges, swarming over her valleys—even in the muddy miles below Chepstow they pour down in a green flood almost to the water, and they make the curving reach which houses Tintern Abbey one of the most beautiful riverside sites in England. If you feel, as I do, that her trees are England's special heritage, you will inevitably regard the Wye as the most beautiful, if not the most lovable of English rivers.

37

But before you make up your mind, you should certainly see the Devon-shire Dart; for this unique river, which in little more than thirty miles changes from a tumbling, brawling, moorland brook into a great estuarial river, can boast of ten miles of the richest scenery in England, scenery which once earned for this manikin of a river the grandiloquent title of the "English Rhine." This famous stretch is from Totnes (the oldest borough in England, having a charter dated 1205) to Dartmouth, and they are miles as rich in historic associations as they are in natural beauty. Even the Wye itself is not lovelier than these great entrenched curves winding between their wooded valleys.

Nevertheless if you visit the Dart, do not forget that other river—the diminutive and often angry torrent "crying" in its narrow bed among the moors; the sunny stream playing among its boulders which might well be that very one of which Lascelles Abercrombie sang :

Make way, make way
You thwarting stones ;
Room for my play,
Serious ones.

Do you not know
My joy at length
Will all wear out
Your solemn strength?

Do you not fear,
O rocks and boulders,
To feel my laughter
On your grave shoulders?

Yet for a while
Thwart me, O boulders;
I need for laughter
Your serious shoulders.

And when my singing
Has razed you quite,
I shall have lost
Half my delight.

The Dart is not alone in its sudden transition from a stream to a great estuary, for nearly all the rivers in this curious south-western peninsula, with its sea coast of some four hundred miles cut off from the rest of England by a land frontier of little more than thirty-five miles, have this same char-acteristic. They are all short; the longest, the Exe, which, rising only a few miles from the Bristol Channel in the north runs into the English Channel in the south, is only fifty-five miles from source to sea, and few others are more than thirty. But almost every one of them, when it reaches the sea,

NET FISHING IN A STREAM
Water colour by Thomas Rowlandson, 1756-1827

opens out into a vast many-tongued estuary and these estuaries have made the West Country. For without this string of land-locked and deep-water harbours, this otherwise cruel and inhospitable coast would have been no place for little ships, and the history of the West Country is the story of her ships and the courage of the men who manned them.

The most famous of these estuarial harbours is the great naval base of Plymouth, which has harboured units of the fleet for centuries and in which Drake and his ships lay in wait for the Armada. Four lovely rivers have helped in its making—the Tamar, Tavy and Lynher from the west and the Plym from the east—but the greatest of these is the Tamar, whose seventy foot deep water channel known as the Hamoaze is one of the wonders of the west. At Saltash it is wider than the Thames at Westminster.

There are so many lovely rivers in these two counties of Devon and Cornwall, and so many scenes whose beauty is world famous, that it is difficult to particularise, but if one were allowed to choose one river only mine would be the Tamar. One would miss much by so doing, and the Teign with its noble gorges would be my own greatest regret, but one would still preserve everything that is typical of a west country river. The Tamar in its comparatively

39

short course shows every aspect of these rivers. From its beginnings as a moorland stream, through precipitous gorges and lovely wooded reaches, to its fitting end as the home of the fleet, it is always picturesque and many of its reaches are as lovely as anything on the Wye.

But though I have long admired these southern rivers, I am not properly qualified to speak of their inland reaches, for I know only the Dart and Tamar and the estuaries well and have seen the others only while motoring about the country. Few of them are navigable even for a canoe (and being mostly fishing rivers are consequently heavily preserved) and since life is short and youth is fleeting, I have usually restricted my explorations to those rivers which can be seen from midstream.

None the less it is right, I think, to consider the west country rivers principally as estuaries, for they are all sea-going rivers and though many of them were anciently harnessed to provide power for mills, their principal importance in the life of the counties has always been as harbours. There has never been much inland navigation, for few of them are easily navigable for more than a score of miles inland. Many of them have ceased to be usable as deep-water harbours in comparatively recent times as a result of the failure of the tides to scour away the detritus brought down by the river, thus forming a shingle bar across its mouth. None the less, many fine harbours remain, and we in this country have little to complain of from the sea, for the tidal wave which sweeps our long coast line has for centuries scoured out the mouths of our rivers and prevented the formation of deltas, and if a little has been lost much has been saved. It is hardly too much to say that our foreign trade was founded jointly on our river mouths and on the tidal wave which keeps them clear.

Even those estuaries which have become closed to shipping still preserve their old link with the sea by providing the finest possible training grounds for future seamen, for their lovely landlocked waters give the best small-boat sailing in the country. But whether you sail or not, it is impossible to help admiring these estuaries, with their sweeping curves and the trees which are everywhere. The ancient name of the city of Exeter is reputed to have been "Kair-Pen-Huel-Goit" which we are told meant "the town at the head of the water in the wood" and this lovely phrase might be used for almost any of the west country estuary towns. Long may they flourish.

The sea has not been as kind to the southern chalk streams as it has to the more westerly rivers of Devon and Cornwall and few of them retain any of their former importance as harbours. The Itchen and the Test indeed run into Southampton Water but they lose their individuality at once in the tidal flood and no-one who sails there can feel that he is on a river. I remember being told, I do not know whether it is still true, that these two rivers were famous as being the only rivers in England on which it was possible to fish for salmon without a rod licence, and this association with fishing in my memory seems to me typical of these southern rivers. For whatever they once were (and we know that many of the forgotten ports at their

BOATS ON THE RIVER BANK, MALDON, ESSEX
Water colour by Wilson Steer, 1933

ON THE TORRIDGE, DEVON
Water colour by Morgan Rendle, 1944
By courtesy of the Artist

mouths were once historically important) they are now best known as the haunt of fishermen. Some of them, particularly the New Forest streams, have a quiet charm, such as that of the little Beaulieu with its fine Abbey, and others have, perhaps, served their purpose in adding to the beauty of the downs by the gaps they have cut in the chalk, but in general they are sluggish and characterless. Possibly I am prejudiced in this, for these rivers are very much preserved and I dislike rivers being made the vehicle of an expensive and exclusive sport. So I must admit that if you like a typical cow-pasture meadow-wandering kind of stream, there are few in England which will please you more than the Arun; and the little Cuckmere has an especial place in my affection as being one of the very few rivers which you can follow right down to the coast and watch making its way out to sea over a few feet of shingly bar, undisturbed by the works of man.

Once the North Foreland is rounded, however, the character of the rivers changes and we are once again in a region of tide-swept estuaries. The Thames and the Medway have already been mentioned, but further up the East Coast is a group of rivers which though no longer the busy and prosperous waterways they once were, are still thronged with ships. For these estuaries, bleak, muddy and uninteresting as they often are, are the yachtsmen's rivers, the home of the little ships of London; and the welcoming waters of Crouch, Chelmer, Blackwater, Colne, Orwell, Stour and Deben have harboured many thousands of the white-sailed craft of a generation whose young men have once again learned the way of a ship with the sea.

But if these Essex and Suffolk rivers resemble the west country rivers in that they are seldom navigable for far inland and so have served more to carry men to the sea than take them inland, that is their only resemblance. For their estuaries, with the possible exception of the Deben which has some fine wooded reaches, are dull to look at (if fascinating to navigate) and their upper reaches are commonplace. Constable has made the Stour world-famous, but even he cannot persuade me that it is anything but a very ordinary and pedestrian kind of stream and the rivers in this part of the country are in general of the kind which one likes only because they are rivers.

Further up the coast from the yachting rivers are three rivers which, although their outlet to the sea is so inconsiderable that a coasting vessel might easily pass it by, are probably among the most famous waterways in the world. It is difficult in this twentieth century to say anything fresh about the Broadland rivers. This curious, almost exotic area, with its three meandering rivers and its innumerable shallow lakes and meres, constitutes the largest inland waterway system in the country—nearly three hundred miles of navigable waters. It is also almost the only one with which the public at large is at all familiar, and the greatest marvel about it all, to me, is that despite the over-advertisement to which it has been subjected, despite the excursions, the motor cruises, the gramophones and the pianos, the Broadland rivers still retain so large a measure of their individuality and charm.

This unique group of waterways is of comparatively recent growth, for at least until Roman times and probably for several centuries later, as the earliest maps show, the three principal rivers, Yare, Bure and Waveney, formed a great estuary at the point where Yarmouth now stands. The rivers were then navigable far inland, and successive waves of invaders penetrated the country by this means. We know, for example, from the Anglo-Saxon Chronicles, that a Danish fleet under King Sweyn sailed up the Yare to Norwich and sacked the city. In the Middle Ages, however, a sandbank formed at the mouth of the estuary, thus excluding the tidal currents and forming a great sheet of water inland behind the barrier. Over the following centuries the deposition of mud and gravel brought down by the rivers has slowly reduced this mass of water to its present form. The process is still continuing and it is probable that within a comparatively short time (historically speaking) the whole of the Broads will become dry land. But they are likely to remain for our time at least as they are now, the haunt of anglers, yachtsmen, artists, writers, anti-quarians, naturalists, bird lovers and the many others to whom this eastern corner of England (a corner in its own way as strangely remote from the rest of the country as are Cornwall and Devon) has an appeal beyond anything to be found elsewhere. Even the most hardened southerner must admit their claim, for these reed-haunted and bird-delighting lakes are unlike anything else in England.

The Broads have another claim to fame as the last home of the inland com-mercial sailing craft. The Norfolk wherries with their enormous boomless mainsails were once a characteristic feature of the landscape and a few still remain, their black sails distinctive among the white-winged yachts. This contrast between old and new is typical of the Broads, for everywhere the pleasure craft is ousting the professional. But though it is fashionable to sneer at Broads sailing, I must confess that I like to see the yachts tacking about the Broads and think they improve rather than disfigure the scene.

Farther north than the Broadland rivers is an almost equally remarkable group of rivers draining into the Wash. The Fenland rivers, Witham, Welland, Nene and Ouse, flow through a great tract of country which is so scarred by man's centuries-old struggle to contain and control the waters of the Wash that it is almost impossible, without a map, to tell where the rivers end and the artificial cuts begin. Even the maps, with their "middle level," "lower level," "ten-mile bottom," and the rest do not do much to make matters clearer.

Before the sea receded, King's Lynn, Wisbech, Spalding and Boston were all busy and prosperous ports, and the Fenland rivers carried a considerable trade far inland—up the Ouse and its tributaries to Cambridge, Bury St. Edmunds and Thetford; up the Nene to Peterborough and Northampton, and the Witham to Lincoln, then almost a port. These early navigations were of supreme importance to the merchants of the Middle Ages, for until the area was properly drained there were no other routes—if you lived in Lincoln and

OLD HOUSES ON THE HIGH BRIDGE, LINCOLN
Water colour by Peter de Wint, 1784-1849

wanted to send your wool to the continent, you either sent it down the Witham or not at all. Even to-day there are few direct roads across the fens. The work of reclamation has closed Lincoln as a port, having cut off its access to the sea, but Boston still has ships at its quaysides and Wisbech on the Nene, greatest of Fenland rivers and still a thriving navigation, has never wholly lost its importance an an inland port, and is to-day the scene of increasing activity. The clearing and extension of the river channels which has been carried out in the present century by the Nene Catchment Board may restore much of their lost prosperity to these ports.

But though the history of these rivers is rich, the landscape which they have created is uniformly uninteresting. The straight lines of the cuts, with their intersecting channels cut neatly across at right angles; the mile upon mile of unending embankment; the uninterrupted flats stretching for miles on either side of the raised roads; the absence of any current, caused by the innumerable locks and sluices—all these combine to give the landscape a most un-English air of straight-jacketed regimentation. There are exceptions, of course; the

43

THE RIVER URE AT SUNDERLAND
Engraving from *Rivers of Great Britain*, 1892

Cam is an obvious one, and I have an affection also for certain stretches of the Little Ouse and the Thet, but in general this is a country whose rivers have been tamed and harnessed to pumping station and power house until they are more the several parts of a vast drainage system than self-respecting rivers. None the less, they are an admirable example of yet another aspect of the importance of rivers, for without them not even Vermuyden could have reclaimed the Fens. They are an example also of how rivers can change a country, for even in the last twenty years the work of drainage and flood control has so changed the landscape as to render parts of it unrecognisable.

Even the Fenland rivers have their moments of relaxation and beauty, but when the Wash is passed we enter a region where the larger rivers know their business and go about it with an air of disillusioned determination. It is singularly in keeping with the contrast between the industrial north and the pasture lands of the south that the larger northern rivers should wear such a grimly utilitarian aspect. But for all their bleak appearances the two great northern estuaries, the Humber on the east and the Mersey on the west, have had an impact on the life of the country which only the Thames can equal. The Humber, in fact, has some claim to be the greatest river in England, for though only thirty-seven miles in length it is one of the eleven major rivers, and two others of that eleven add their waters to its own—for the Humber is no natural river but simply the name given to the confluence of the Yorkshire Ouse and

44

the Trent. In point of size alone, it is impressive, for it is a mile across at the beginning of its life and gradually increases in width, until at Grimsby it is four miles across. Its port of Hull is the third in England and the inland water traffic which uses its estuary, linked as it is with the Severn, Mersey and Thames, is second to none. But it is a swift and treacherous waterway, dangerous for small boats, and though it boasts a flourishing yacht club can hardly be regarded as a pleasurable river. It is one to be respected and admired rather than loved.

If the Humber is remarkable as being a river without a source, the Mersey is equally remarkable as being a river without a history, for no mention of it occurs in any record earlier than the eleventh century, and it is even then only referred to in passing as a boundary. The estuary of the Dee was formerly of greater importance and it was not until this silted up that the Mersey came into its own. To-day the Mersey, with its tributary the Irwell, is probably the busiest inland waterway in the world. Its port of Liverpool is the second in the country and Manchester at the head of the great Ship Canal formed from the waters of the Mersey and the Irwell, is one of the most thriving industrial towns of the north. Manchester in fact owes the greater part of its early prosperity to waterways, for this north-west corner of England is one of the very few places in which one can feel that the rivers and canals are still a vital part of the life of the people. It is impressive to watch a barge train steaming up the Trent, but it is awe-inspiring to see a towering ocean-going steamer locking up the canal to Manchester, or watch the Bridgewater Canal being swung aside bodily to allow a ten thousand ton tanker to pass beneath on the Ship Canal.

Farther north than either of these two rivers is another grimly practical estuary—Milton's "Coaly Tyne," traditional home of the coasting colliers, and still probably second only to the Thames in the number of vessels which use it. Tyneside has something of the same fascination as London river in its ceaseless maritime activity, for no waterway which is so thronged with ships and their associated activities can ever be dull; but it has been so much more industrialised that it is more of a vast tidal dock than a river. From Newcastle to the sea its banks are crowded with shipyards, chemical factories, engineering works, glass-works, and every possible kind of factory or warehouse. In prosperous times these twelve miles must be one of the busiest and most populous waterways in the world, but they wore a gloomy, bleak and dispirited air when I last saw them some years before the war. Let us hope that all that is now changed and for ever.

Despite the utilitarian aspect of its tidal portion the upper Tyne is a swift, clear and most pleasant stream. The change from estuary to river is abrupt, for as soon as the tidal limit is reached its character changes, and it becomes a broad shallow river, running in a rocky bed with little hindrance (for there are few weirs). It is indeed, particularly in its upper reaches, a most attractive river, with its swift shallow stretches alternating with deep and quiet pools,

45

and it has something in common with the Devon rivers in its transition from a wild moorland stream to a deep-water estuary—though it is a far cry from the west country estuaries to the Tyne.

It is an abrupt transition from the industrial waterways of the north to the swift-running mountain streams which are my real love among English rivers, but I have left them until the last not only because it is a natural human instinct to leave the most pleasant things to the end, but also because they cannot conveniently be considered geographically. For they are to be found in all parts of the country; from the Eden in the extreme north to the Tamar in the south the country is honeycombed with them. Many of these rapid rivers become civilised and navigable in their lower reaches—one of them, the Ribble has in recent times become a notable example of modern river navigations—for few of them, like the little Rheidol which seems almost to fling itself into the sea, remain rapid for their whole course. But all of them in their upper reaches are pure elemental river, untouched by man, still living in the geological past when the rivers were shaping England. For her mountain rivers are shaping England still, abrading her rocks, deepening and widening her valleys, and a man with imagination can see near the sources of such rivers what the land must have looked like when it was being made.

If any man loves rivers let him take a train and hunt out the sources of any of these rivers, and explore their upper reaches—Eden, Usk, Wharfe, Swale, Teifi, Tees, Ribble, Dee, Derwent, Lune—and he will see some of the finest scenery in England and waterfalls and gorges such as few people imagine to exist in this country.

There is much else that I should like to say about rapid rivers—but this is no place for a disquisition on wild-water canoeing, that most fascinating of all sports which, typically enough, was invented by the English, forgotten by them, adopted by the continental nations and only recently re-introduced into this country. But whether you love them for the scenery they make, or for the sport they give, the rapid rivers should always be remembered as the beginning of things. All our rivers were once like this, and it is good to remember our past and envisage our future in the working of such rivers.

IV

Viam qui nescit, qua deveniat ad mare,
Eum oportet amnem quaerere comitem sibi   PLAUTUS

*(He who knows not the way leading to the sea
should make the river his companion)*

IT may seem strange that a book on the English rivers should end with a reference to the sea, but all rivers come at last to the sea and so should a book on rivers. For, as has been said before, the only proper business of a river is to carry men to the sea, and it is our contention that the English rivers have excelled all others in this respect.

WHERRIES ON THE YARE
Oil painting by J. S. Cotman, 1782-1842

If you look at even a very small map of England, it will be seen as a small area of land with a vast coast line which is cut into by the mouths of innumerable rivers. These rivers radiate inland in such a way that, place a man where you will, from Land's End to the Tyne, he need seldom walk more than a few miles in any direction without striking the bank of a river or stream which will lead him to the sea. When he has found that river in all probability there will be other men on it already, "messing about with boats." Wherever you go in England, from the bleak waters of the north to the Riviera-like estuaries of Devon and Cornwall, you will find boats on the river, and these boats are yet another way in which rivers have helped to make England great. For the rivers have been for centuries the training ground for future seamen, and every man who learns to sail on a river sooner or later finds his way to the sea. From the west country estuaries, to the Solent, the Thames, the east coast havens, even to the inhospitable Humber, the little ships in their thousands cluster round England like a brood of nurslings which for all their air of casualness spring instantly to her defence in time of trouble. Inland, too, on the Broads, the lakes, and any river wide enough to permit a small vessel to come about, you will find the ships of this nation of amateur seamen. The boy who sails a home-made canvas canoe on his local canal and the yachtsman

47

with his sleek Bermudan sloop at Burnham-on-Crouch are one in spirit. They are the men who want to adventure on water, and the greatness of England has been founded on that spirit. In times of peace it takes her merchant-adventurers round the globe, and in times of war it has always provided that emergency reserve of seamen which has for long been the secret of this country's power to double her navy overnight. The men who loved rivers yesterday are manning her warships to-day, and many a motor gunboat or torpedo boat now at sea will end her days as an engineless hulk moored by a riverside garden.

THE COURSE OF THE WARWICKSHIRE AVON

SHORT BIBLIOGRAPHY

Rapid Rivers, 1935, *The Heart of England by Waterway*, 1933, and *Canoeing* (a comprehensive guide to rivers and canals and the art of voyaging on them) 1936, all by William Bliss.—*Rivers of the South*, 1938, by A. B. Austin and J. Dixon Scott.—*Handbook and Guide to British Waterways* : British Canoe Association.—*Our Waterways*, 1906, by V. A. Forbes and W. H. R. Ashford. —*Narrow Boat*, 1944, by L. T. C. Rolt.—*The Flower of Gloster*, 1911, by E. Temple Thurston.—*A Caravan Afloat*, *c*. 1900, by C. J. Auberton.—*Bradshaws Canals and Navigable Rivers of England and Wales*, 1928, edited by H. R. de Salis.—*Canals and Inland Waterways*, 1929, by G. Cadbury and S. P. Dobbs. *Historical Account of the Navigable Rivers, Canals and Railways Throughout Great Britain*, 1831, by Joseph Priestley.—*Inland Waterways of Great Britain*, 1939, by W. Eric Wilson